.50

D1716343

Voting in an Election

John Hamilton

ABDO
Publishing Company

visit us at
www.abdopub.com

Published by ABDO Publishing Company, 4940 Viking Drive, Edina, Minnesota 55435.
Copyright © 2005 by Abdo Consulting Group, Inc. International copyrights reserved in all
countries. No part of this book may be reproduced in any form without written permission from
the publisher. The Checkerboard Library™ is a trademark and logo of ABDO Publishing
Company.

Printed in the United States.

Cover Photos: Corbis
Interior Photos: AP/Wide World pp. 18, 19, 20; Corbis pp. 1, 5, 7, 10, 15, 31;
    Getty Images pp. 9, 12, 13, 14, 17, 21, 23, 29

Series Coordinator: Kristin Van Cleaf
Editors: Kate A. Conley, Stephanie Hedlund
Art Direction & Maps: Neil Klinepier

Library of Congress Cataloging-in-Publication Data

Hamilton, John, 1959-
    Voting in an election / John Hamilton.
        p. cm. -- (Government in action!)
    Includes index.
    ISBN 1-59197-647-2
    1. Elections--United States--Juvenile literature. 2. Voting--United States--Juvenile literature.
    [1. Elections. 2. Voting.] I. Title. II. Government in action! (ABDO Publishing Company)

JK1978.H35 2004
324.6'3'0973--dc22

2003070811

Contents

Every Vote Counts!

One of the most important parts of a **democratic** government is the election process. It allows people to decide important issues by voting on them. This keeps citizens involved in their government.

In the United States, the **Constitution** grants citizens the right to vote. They elect leaders at all government levels. This allows power to transfer peacefully from one leader to the next. Elections are not limited to the government. Corporations use elections to choose officers. Unions vote on leaders. Students even hold elections to choose student body positions.

When Americans vote, they are exercising their freedoms. However, Americans know that voting is also a responsibility. It shapes the nation's future. For this reason, every vote counts!

Opposite page: A boy practices voting in a presidential primary election.

By the People

Elections are not an entirely new idea. They can be found throughout history. For example in ancient Greece, public officers were often chosen through voting. However, only a select group of people had the right to vote.

For hundreds of years after this, **dictators** or monarchs often ruled. Some rulers used force to take political power. Others believed God had given them the right to rule. During this time, elections did not disappear. But, it was mostly those who were rich, powerful, or connected to the church who could vote.

Eventually, the idea of **democracy** began to redevelop. In the 1600s and 1700s, philosophers such as John Locke and Jean-Jacques Rousseau believed all citizens had **civil rights**. One of these rights was universal **suffrage.**

The American **Revolutionary War** put this idea to the test. After the war, a larger representation of the public chose the new country's leaders. Eventually, suffrage was expanded. Now, all races and genders are allowed to vote.

Many people around the world thought American **democracy** would fail. They didn't think the people could govern themselves. But after more than 200 years, the United States has shown that self-rule can work.

Voting rights have not always been enjoyed by all citizens. In 1920, protesters called suffragettes won the right to vote for women in the United States.

Free to Choose

The United States is a representative **democracy**. This means citizens choose officials to represent them in the government. So, Americans have control over how their country is run.

The people exercise control by voting in elections. As a group, voters are called the electorate. The electorate has a choice of candidates for each position. No one can force a voter to choose a specific candidate. People are free to select who they think will do the best job.

Americans vote using the Australian ballot system. This means that voters make their choices secretly. Votes are cast in booths where no one else can watch. This keeps people from feeling pressured by interest groups or politicians. It also helps keep elections fair.

Citizens vote for national leaders such as the president and members of Congress. They elect their state's governor and legislators. Americans can even choose their local mayor and city council members. Usually, people from specific political parties fill these positions.

Citizens mark their ballots in private booths so that their votes will be kept secret.

INSTRUCTION FOR THE GUIDANCE OF VOTERS

GENERAL ELECTION OF NOVEMBER 7, 2000

PURPOSE OF THE GENERAL ELECTION

The Polls will be Open from 6:00 A.M. to 7:00 P.M.

MANNER OF VOTING:

HOW TO USE THE VOTE RECORDER:

PROCEDURE FOR WRITE-IN VOTES:

VOTER ASSISTANCE:

VOTERS ARE NOT PERMITTED TO DO ANY OF THE FOLLOWING:

Political Parties

In a **democracy**, people with similar political beliefs work together in political parties. This idea is not new. It first developed in Britain in the 1600s.

Today, two parties have the most influence in U.S. politics. Republicans tend to be conservative and favor less government control. Democrats are more liberal and prefer a strong central government.

Other parties also exist in the United States. They are often called third parties. Just a few are the Libertarian, Progressive, and Green parties. Often, these groups have specific goals. No third party has yet won a presidential election, but they have influenced elections and policies.

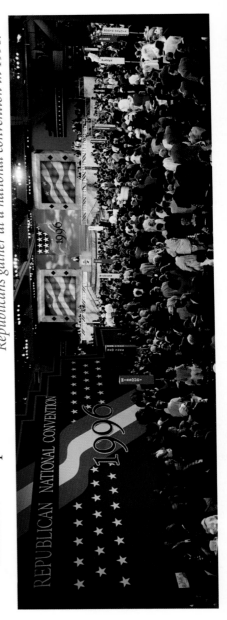

Republicans gather at a national convention in 1996.

All political parties work to get their candidates elected. They know that when many of a party's members are elected, the party has more control. This affects the kinds of laws that are passed. To do this, a party must first convince the voters that its candidates are the best choice.

The elephant and the donkey are traditional symbols for the Republican and Democratic parties.

Republican

Democrat

Selecting Candidates

During the election process, citizens have a responsibility. It is to learn as much as they can about the candidates and the issues. This is an important part of a free **democracy**.

Voters must be informed in order to make meaningful choices. Often, the electorate learns about the candidates through campaigns. Campaigns advertise a candidate's positions on the issues. They also give voters a glimpse of a candidate's personality.

Candidates campaign by creating television commercials, print and radio ads, and posters. They make appearances at events in order to meet the public. They also set up rallies and public meetings to speak about the issues.

A campaign poster advertises the Democratic Party's candidates in the 1984 U.S. presidential election.

The candidates **debate** important political issues, too. These debates, especially for national offices such as the presidency, are often aired on television. So, watching debates is another good way to learn about the candidates' positions.

Early in an election, several candidates from the same party may campaign for one position. But usually each party only officially supports one candidate in the general election. Voters can choose this candidate in either a caucus or a primary.

Wesley Clark campaigns for nomination as his party's presidential candidate.

A caucus is a private meeting of party members. During this meeting, people discuss the issues and the candidates. Then they nominate a candidate.

Today most states hold primaries instead of caucuses. Primaries can be either direct or indirect. In a direct primary, the people cast votes for the candidate they wish to see run in the general election.

In an indirect primary, voters choose delegates who are dedicated to their candidate. The delegates then go to a national convention. There, they choose the party's candidate. This method is often used in presidential primaries.

Iowans meet at a caucus to discuss their party's candidates.

I HEREBY DECLARE MY PREFERENCE
FOR CANDIDATE FOR THE OFFICE OF
PRESIDENT OF THE UNITED STATES
TO BE AS FOLLOWS:

KATHERINE BATEMAN
Chicago, Illinois

CAROL MOSELEY BRAUN
Chicago, Illinois

HARRY W. BRAUN III
Phoenix, Arizona

WILLIE FELIX CARTER
Fort Worth, Texas

WESLEY K. CLARK
Little Rock, Arkansas

"RANDY" CROW
Wilmington, North Carolina

HOWARD DEAN
Burlington, Vermont

GERRY DOKKA
Atlanta, Georgia

JOHN EDWARDS
Raleigh, North Carolina

"DICK" GEPHARDT
St. Louis, Missouri

MILDRED GLOVER
Baltimore, Maryland

VINCENT S. HAMM
Golden, Colorado

JOHN F. KERRY
Boston, Massachusetts

CAROLINE PETTINATO KILLEEN
Scranton, Pennsylvania

DENNIS J. KUCINICH
Cleveland, Ohio

LYNDON H. LAROUCHE, JR.
Round Hill, Virginia

R. RANDY LEE
New York, New York

"JOE" LIEBERMAN
New Haven, Connecticut

ROBERT H. LINNELL
Lebanon, New Hampshire

EDWARD THOMAS O'DONNELL, JR.
Lebanon, New Hampshire

FERN PENNA
Kingston, New York

"AL" SHARPTON
Brooklyn, New York

LEONARD DENNIS TALBOW
Scottsdale, Arizona

WRITE-IN

Primaries are either closed or open. In a closed primary, only people who are registered members of a particular political party may vote. In an open primary, citizens do not have to be official party members. Closed primaries are more common than open primaries.

Choosing a party's candidate in a caucus or primary narrows down the choices. Next, the candidates run in a general election. Americans vote to support their candidate and their own ideas on how the government should be run. But first, they must register.

The ballot for the New Hampshire primary election shows all of the Democratic Party's candidates.

Registering

People are allowed to vote only once in an election. They must also be qualified to vote. So before doing so, U.S. citizens must register.

To register, citizens have to meet certain requirements. A person must be age 18 or older. He or she must also be mentally competent. Some people, such as convicted felons, are not allowed to vote.

Another requirement for registration is residency. A citizen must live in the state where he or she is voting. The person's address determines his or her voting **precinct** and **polling place.**

Each state has slightly different rules about how to register. In most states, voters may mail in their registration. However in Wyoming, voters must register in person. And in North Dakota, voters are not required to register at all!

Some states stop registering people a certain number of days before an election. In other states, people can register on Election Day. Then, they are ready to vote.

A citizen registers to vote by filling out the official form.

Election Day

On Election Day, citizens go to their **polling place** to vote. In most states they show identification. The poll worker checks each citizen's name off on a list of registered voters. This prevents people from voting more than once.

What happens next depends on the voting system. Most often, the person is given a ballot. This sheet of paper lists all of the candidates for all of the open positions. Voters mark the ballot in a private booth. They usually either fill in a box or arrow, or punch out a hole next to their choices.

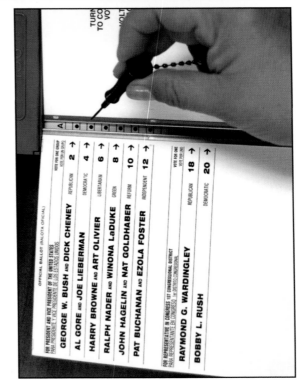

Punch card ballots are usually slid into holders. The voter punches holes next to his or her choices in order to cast each vote.

When finished, voters place their ballots in a closed box. Or, more often today, they put their ballots into a machine. The machine scans and counts the votes automatically.

Some **polling places**

don't use paper ballots. Instead, a voter enters a booth and closes a curtain. Inside, the voter flips levers to indicate for whom he or she is voting. The machine records the votes, and then it resets itself for the next voter.

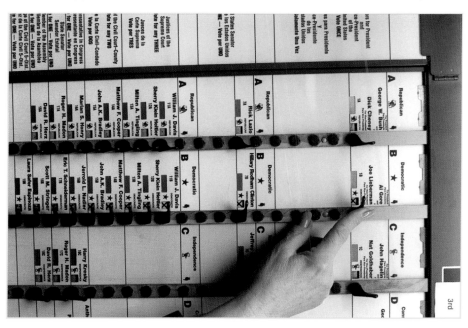

With a mechanical lever voting machine, there is no ballot. Instead, the voter flips levers next to his or her choices. These machines are not as common today as they once were.

The newest voting technology uses computers. The names of the candidates appear on a screen. The person touches the screen to cast a vote. The information is then recorded on a disk. This method is still being studied to make sure it is both safe and **accurate.**

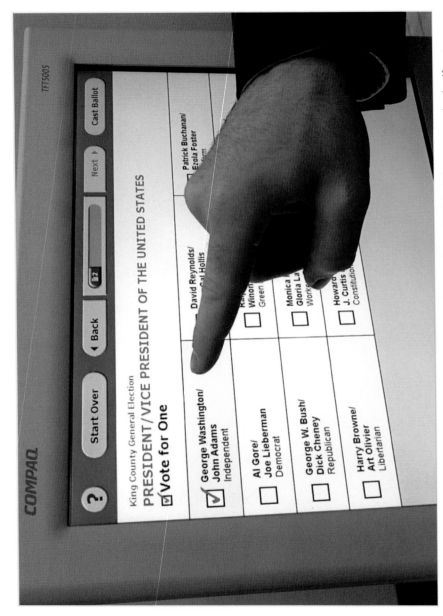

Voting by computer is called direct recording electronic, or DRE. This system is similar to the old mechanical lever machines. The voter makes choices directly on a computer screen.

Sometimes, voters cannot make it to their **polling place** on Election Day. For example, soldiers might be stationed overseas. And, students might live in other states while attending school. These people may vote by absentee ballot. This ballot is filled out and mailed in before the general election.

Polling stations are usually open from about six or seven in the morning until seven or eight in the evening. After the polls close, election officials count all the votes, including the absentee votes. Next the results are certified, and a winner is declared.

Absentee ballots are bundled for storage after an election.

Sometimes it can take several days to count and certify all the votes. However, the media usually predicts the winners soon after voting ends. They use scientific polling, or exit surveys, to find out for whom people voted.

Different types of elections can be held on Election Day. For example, a general election may be held to choose leaders. Or, citizens may vote on certain laws or **constitutional amendments.**

General elections are spaced out depending on the position being filled. For example, the people elect members of the House of Representatives every two years. Presidential elections are held every four years. National general elections are held on the first Tuesday after the first Monday in November.

Sometimes, no candidate receives an **absolute majority** of votes. In this case, some states will hold a runoff. In this type of election, the two candidates with the most votes run against each other.

Even after the general election, voters still play a part. Recall elections are sometimes held to remove people from office before their term is up. This can happen if the **incumbent** commits a crime. Or, the electorate may be unhappy with how the incumbent is doing his or her job.

In addition, special elections can be held if there is a need. For example, an **incumbent** may retire or die. A special election would then be held to fill the position. Citizens may also vote to approve laws dealing with current events.

In 2003, California governor Gray Davis was voted out of office in a recall election.

The Electoral College

In most cases, the election is over after Election Day. However, the U.S. presidential election is different. Though the general election is in November, the winner is not official until January.

This happens because the presidential election is indirect. Voters actually choose **electors**, rather than the president. In turn, the electors meet and vote on the nation's next leader.

Each state has a different number of electors. This number is equal to the number of members each state has in the U.S. Congress. Together, these electors are called the Electoral College.

The Electoral College meets in December. At that time, the electors cast their votes for president and vice president. They usually base their votes on how the people of their home states voted. In January, Congress counts the votes. The candidate with the **absolute majority** of votes wins.

This system was created by the **Founding Fathers**. They recognized that direct elections aren't always ideal. They worried about giving the people too much power. There was also concern that small states wouldn't have as much power as the larger states. For these reasons, they formed the Electoral College.

2004 Electoral Votes for Each State

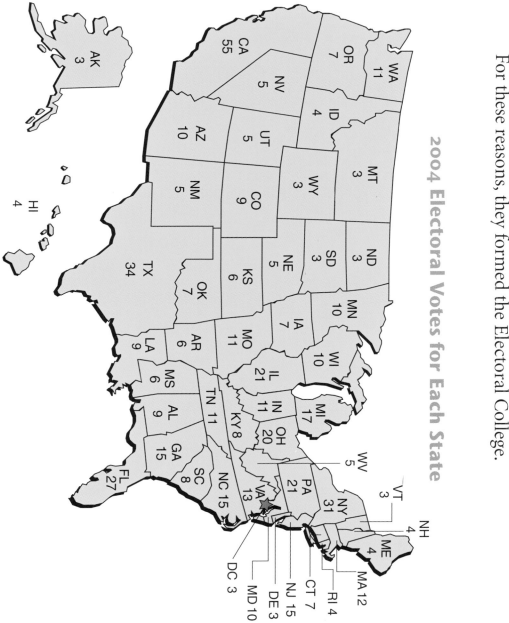

AK 3

HI 4

WA 11
OR 7
CA 55
NV 5
ID 4
MT 3
AZ 10
UT 5
WY 3
NM 5
CO 9
ND 3
SD 3
NE 5
KS 6
OK 7
TX 34
MN 10
IA 7
MO 11
AR 6
LA 9
MS 6
AL 9
TN 11
KY 8
IL 21
WI 10
IN 11
MI 17
OH 20
GA 15
SC 8
NC 15
FL 27
VA 13
WV 5
PA 21
NY 31
VT 3
NH 4
ME 4
MA 12
RI 4
CT 7
NJ 15
DE 3
MD 10
DC 3

UNUSUAL U.S. ELECTIONS

The election process doesn't always turn out as expected. A number of times in U.S. history the candidate with the most popular votes has still lost the election. Each time, special circumstances caused the unusual results.

1824

In the election of 1824, four candidates received electoral votes. Andrew Jackson received 99, John Quincy Adams 84, William H. Crawford 41, and Henry Clay 37. Since no one had an absolute majority, the House of Representatives was required to elect the president from the top three candidates. Adams was chosen over Jackson. Clay was Speaker of the House and voted for Adams. In addition, Adams later appointed Clay secretary of state. For this reason, many people felt the election had been unfair.

1888

In the 1888 election, Democratic presidential candidate Grover Cleveland won the popular vote by nearly 100,000 votes. However, when the Electoral College voted, Cleveland received 168 votes and Benjamin Harrison received 233. Harrison became president.

2000

In 2000, the vote was very close between Al Gore and George W. Bush. In Florida, the punch card system caused problems, and poll workers started recounting the votes by hand. After five weeks, the U.S. Supreme Court decided to end the recount in Florida, which meant that George W. Bush had won. Since then it has been determined that Gore actually won the popular vote, though Bush won the electoral vote.

Since 2000, several bills have been introduced in Congress. Lawmakers want to avoid problems such as those in 2000 in the future. Many states are upgrading polling machines and making sure procedures are more fair and consistent.

A Single Vote

Americans have many rights that people in other countries do not have. With these rights come certain responsibilities. Voting in elections is one of these responsibilities.

Elections are how Americans participate in their government. Voting allows them to create and support government policies. It is a way to express satisfaction or dissent with their government representatives. Without elections, the United States's way of government wouldn't work.

Even though it is their responsibility, many people don't vote. They don't think their single vote matters. But many elections have been decided by just a few votes. In California in 1911, women gained the right to vote by only one vote in each **precinct**.

Even if a candidate doesn't win, even one vote still shows support for that person's political views. Remember, one vote can make a difference!

A boy helps his mother vote by translating the ballot from English into her native language.

Glossary

absolute majority - more than half of a total.

accurate - free of errors.

amendment - a change to a country's constitution.

civil - of or relating to the relationship between a government and its citizens.

Constitution - the laws that govern the United States.

debate - to discuss a question or topic, often publicly.

democracy - a governmental system in which people vote on how to run their country.

dictator - a ruler with complete control who usually governs in a cruel or unfair way.

elector - someone who represents a group of people in a vote.

Founding Fathers - the men who attended the Constitutional Convention in Philadelphia in 1787. They helped write the U.S. Constitution.

incumbent - the person currently holding a certain office.

polling place - the site where votes are cast in an election.

precinct - a smaller part of a county or town used in elections.

Revolutionary War - from 1775 to 1783. A war for independence between Britain and its North American colonies. The colonists won and created the United States of America.

suffrage - the right to vote.

Web Sites

To learn more about elections, visit ABDO Publishing Company on the World Wide Web at **www.abdopub.com**. Web sites about voting and elections are featured on our Book Links page. These links are routinely monitored and updated to provide the most current information available.

Index

A
Australian ballot system 8

B
ballots 18, 19, 21

C
campaigning 12, 13
candidates 8, 11, 12, 13, 14, 15, 18, 20, 22, 24, 28
caucuses 13, 14, 15
Congress, U.S. 8, 22, 24
Constitution, U.S. 4, 22

D
debates 13

E
Election Day 16, 18, 21, 22, 24
Electoral College 24, 25

electorate 8, 12, 22
exit surveys 22

F
Founding Fathers 25

G
Great Britain 10
Greece 6

H
history 6, 7, 28

L
Locke, John 6

P
political parties 8, 10, 11, 13, 14, 15
polling place 16, 18, 19, 21
primaries 13, 14, 15

R
registration 15, 16, 18
requirements 16
Revolutionary War 6
rights 4, 6, 16, 28
Rousseau, Jean-Jacques 6

S
suffrage 6, 28

T
types of elections 4, 14, 15, 22, 23

V
voting systems 18, 19, 20, 21, 24, 25

32